Planets in Our Solar System

SATURN

by Steve Foxe

PEBBLE
a capstone imprint

Pebble Explore is published by Pebble, an imprint of Capstone.
1710 Roe Crest Drive
North Mankato, Minnesota 56003
www.capstonepub.com

Library of Congress Cataloging-in-Publication Data is available on the Library of Congress website.
ISBN 978-1-9771-2396-1 (hardcover)
ISBN 978-1-9771-2696-2 (paperback)
ISBN 978-1-9771-2433-3 (eBook PDF)

Summary: Saturn is famous for its rings. This very windy planet has another claim to fame—it has the most moons of all eight planets! Discover more amazing facts about the sixth planet in the solar system!

Image Credits
Bridgeman Images: Giancarlo Costa, 5; iStockphoto: LYagovy, 18–19; NASA: JPL/Space Science Institute, 12, 18, 23, 24, The Hubble Heritage Team (STScI/AURA)Acknowledgment: R.G. French (Wellesley College), J. Cuzzi (NASA/Ames), L. Dones (SwRI), and J. Lissauer (NASA/Ames), 10–11; Science Source: ATLAS PHOTO BANK, 27, Science Source, 26, Shigemi Numazawa/Atlas Photo Bank, 25; Shutterstock: 3000ad, 17, Andamati, 22, bluecrayola, 16, Dima Zel, 4, Dotted Yeti, Cover Left, Kirschner, 20, Macrovector, 9, MarcelClemens, Back Cover, 1, Meilun, 6 Bottom, Mustafa Bulent Keskin, 21, NASA images, Cover, Sebastian Kaulitzki, 6 Top, Tristan3D, 7, Vytautas Kielaitis, 28, zombiu26, 14–15; Wikimedia: Sun image: HalloweenNight/Gas giants images: NASA/JPL (Jupiter image by Björn Jónsson) Image modified by PlanetUser, 13

Design Elements
Shutterstock: Arcady, BLACKDAY, ebes, LynxVector, phipatbig, Stefan Holm, veronchick_84

Editorial Credits
Editor: Kristen Mohn; Designer: Jennifer Bergstrom; Media Researcher: Tracy Cummins; Production Specialist: Tori Abraham

All internet sites appearing in back matter were available and accurate when this book was sent to press.

Table of Contents

Words in **bold** are in the glossary.

Saturn, the Extreme Planet

Saturn is a special planet in our **solar system**. It has unusual rings. It has an odd shape. The planet is special in other ways too.

Roman god Saturn

Saturn is one of five planets you can see without a telescope. It is the farthest planet you can see with your eyes. People have known about Saturn for thousands of years. Long ago, Romans named the planet after their god Saturn.

Saturn is very large. But it is very light for its size. The planet would float like a beach ball in a giant bathtub!

Earth   Saturn   Jupiter

About 760 Earths could fit inside Saturn. Jupiter is the only planet bigger than Saturn. Saturn and Jupiter are alike in many ways.

Big Saturn also has big storms and strong winds. This planet has some of the fastest winds in the solar system!

Long Years and Short Days

There are eight planets in our solar system. Saturn is the sixth planet from the sun. Earth is the third planet. The planets go around the sun. Their paths are called **orbits.**

It takes Saturn about 29 years to circle the sun! One year is how long Earth takes to circle the sun. Saturn goes around the sun only about three times during a person's life.

Mercury

Jupiter

Venus

Earth

Uranus

Neptune

Mars

Saturn

Orbit paths of each planet

During orbit, planets spin. Saturn spins faster than Earth. It spins one time in 10 hours and 42 minutes. That means Saturn's day is less than 11 hours long. A day on Earth is 24 hours.

Saturn's fast spin changes its shape. Its top and bottom are flatter. It is like a ball that has lost some air. This happens to Jupiter too. But Saturn is the flattest planet in the solar system.

11

A Gas Giant

Saturn cannot support life. It has no air to breathe. It has no ground to stand on! The planet is made up of **gases**. Saturn and Jupiter are both called **gas giants.** There are other gas giants outside of our solar system. Most are close to their suns.

Gases around Saturn

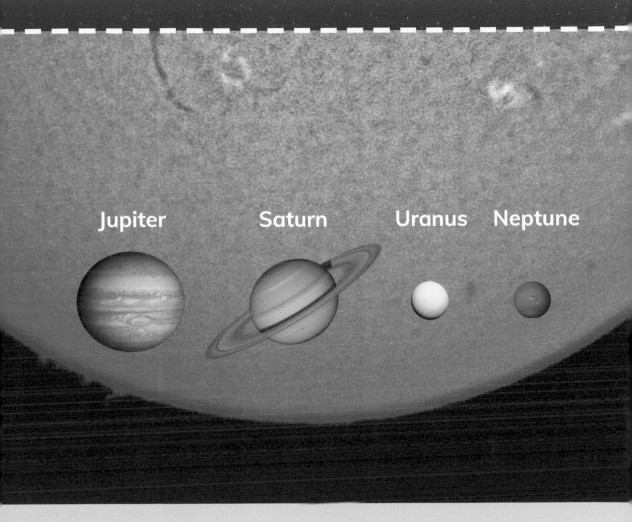

Jupiter   **Saturn**   **Uranus**   **Neptune**

Gas giants and ice giants

Some people also call Neptune and Uranus gas giants. Others call them **ice giants**. Their gases have turned to ice.

There is a hard, rocky **core** at the center of Saturn. It is about the size of Earth. A force called **pressure** affects the core. It makes the gases hot and thick. The gases become liquid and metal.

Saturn's core is very hot. Heat makes **energy**. Saturn makes more energy than it gets from the sun. Saturn's core is even hotter than the sun! Scientists are trying to learn why Saturn's core is so hot.

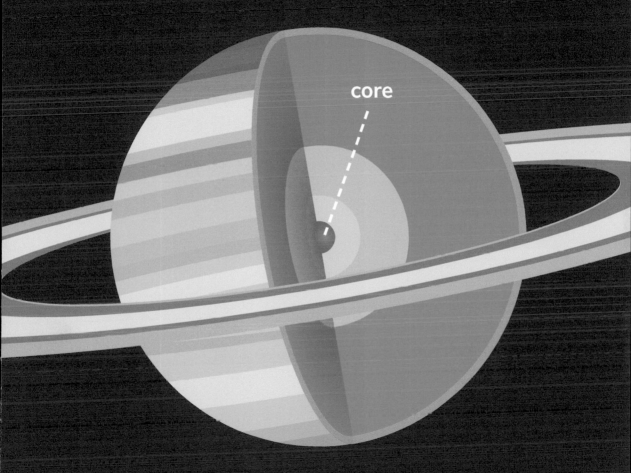

Saturn's Wild Rings

Saturn is famous for its rings. Other planets have rings too. Saturn's rings are easiest to see. They are made up of things in space that broke apart. The broken pieces began circling Saturn.

Dust bits in Saturn's rings

Some of the pieces are small bits of dust. Others are as big as tall buildings. Each ring has billions of pieces.

The rings are very thin. But they stretch out far from Saturn. They reach as far as from Earth to the moon!

Saturn's rings have seven parts. They are named after letters in the alphabet. A and B were discovered first. They are easiest to see. Most of the rings are close together. There is one big gap between parts A and B.

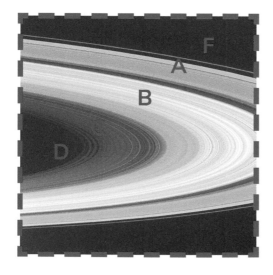

Each ring moves around Saturn at
a different speed. Saturn's rings seem
to disappear about every 14 years.
That is when their thinnest sides point
toward Earth.

A Planet with Many Moons

Earth has one moon. Saturn has 82 moons! Some moons circle Saturn inside its rings. Others circle farther out.

Moons around Saturn

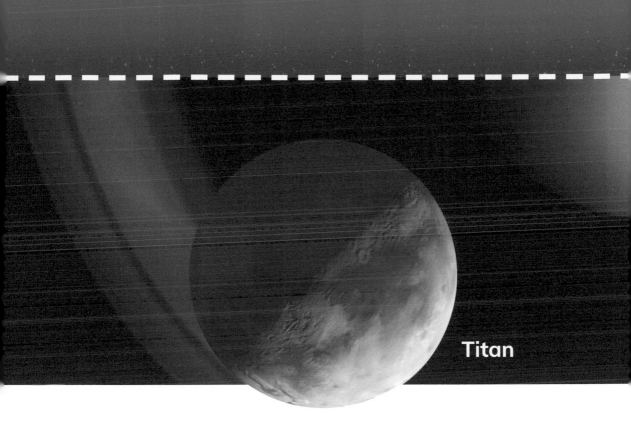

Titan

Titan is Saturn's largest moon. It is larger than the planet Mercury. Titan is very cold. It gets very little heat from the sun.

Titan and Enceladus are Saturn's special moons. They have ice and water. Life as we know it could not happen there now. But some scientists think these moons could have life someday.

Rhea

Rhea is Saturn's second-biggest
moon. But it is not very big. It is smaller
than Earth's moon. Rhea is icy. It has
many **craters**.

Not all of Saturn's moons are round. Some are shaped like a potato! Saturn's moons come in many sizes. Some are as small as a sports stadium.

Saturn has more moons than any other planet. Not all of them have names yet. Scientists discovered 20 of Saturn's moons in 2019.

Saturn's moon Hyperion

Studying Strange Saturn

A strange storm sits at Saturn's north pole. Strong winds create a shape with six sides. It is much bigger than Earth's hurricanes. There is no other storm like it in the solar system.

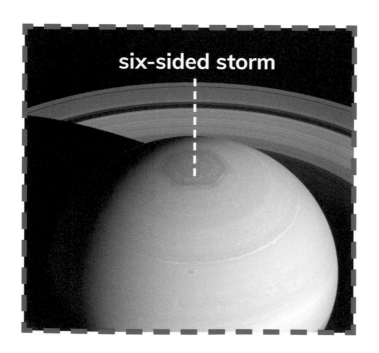

six-sided storm

A probe explores Saturn.

Probes helped us discover Saturn's storm. **NASA** has sent four probes to Saturn. The first probe went to Saturn in 1979. The next two probes flew by Saturn in 1980 and 1981.

Cassini probe was named for early astronomer Giovanni Cassini.

We learned a lot about Saturn from the Cassini probe. It launched in 1997. It reached Saturn in 2004. Cassini circled the planet for 13 years. Cassini also carried a smaller probe. It landed on Titan.

Cassini finished its work in 2017. It fell into Saturn's storms on purpose. The probe sent NASA information until it broke apart.

Probe landing on Titan

Cassini taught us much about Saturn. But there is still more to learn. Saturn's rings and storms hold many secrets. Maybe one day you will help discover more about this special planet!

Fast Facts

Name:
Saturn

Location:
6th planet from the sun

Planet Type:
gas giant

Discovered:
Ancient people spotted Saturn in the
night sky. Galileo Galilei was the first
to see it with a telescope in 1610.

Moons:
82

Glossary

core (KOR)—the inner part of a planet or a dwarf planet that is made of metal or rock

crater (KRAY-tur)—a large hole in the ground caused by crashing rocks

energy (EN-ur-jee)—power, such as making things move or making light or heat

gas (GASS)—something that is not solid or liquid and does not have a definite shape

gas giant (GASS JYE-unt)—a large planet made up mostly of gases

ice giant (ICE JYE-unt)—a planet made up mostly of ice and liquids

NASA (NA-suh)—National Aeronautics and Space Administration, which runs the U.S. space program

orbit (OR-bit)—the path an object follows while circling an object in space

pressure (PRESH-ur)—the force made by pressing on something

probe (PROHB)—a small vehicle used to explore objects in outer space

solar system (SOH-lur SISS-tuhm)—the sun and the objects that move around it

telescope (TEL-uh-skope)—a tool people use to look at objects in space

Read More

Baines, Becky. *Planets*. Washington, D.C.: National Geographic Kids, 2016.

Radomski, Kassandra. *The Secrets of Saturn*. North Mankato, MN: Capstone Press, 2016.

Rathburn, Betsy. *Saturn*. Minneapolis: Bellwether Media, 2019.

Internet Sites

10 Facts about Space!
https://www.natgeokids.com/nz/discover/science/space/ten-facts-about-space/

Saturn Facts for Kids
http://www.sciencekids.co.nz/sciencefacts/planets/saturn.html

NASA Kids' Club
https://www.nasa.gov/kidsclub/index.html

Index